THAT'S ONE DAMN SEXY APE

GAVIN ROACH

CURRENCY PRESS
The performing arts publisher

CURRENT THEATRE SERIES

First published in 2024
by Currency Press Pty Ltd,
Gadigal Land, Suite 310, 46–56 Kippax Street, Surry Hills, NSW 2010, Australia
enquiries@currency.com.au
www.currency.com.au

in association with Gavin Roach Presents

Copyright: *That's One Damn Sexy Ape* © Gavin Roach, 2024.

COPYING FOR EDUCATIONAL PURPOSES

The Australian *Copyright Act 1968* [Act] allows a maximum of one chapter or 10% of this book, whichever is the greater, to be copied by any educational institution for its educational purposes provided that that educational institution [or the body that administers it] has given a remuneration notice to Copyright Agency [CA] under the Act. For details of the CA licence for educational institutions contact CA, 12/66 Goulburn Street, Sydney, NSW, 2000; tel: within Australia 1800 066 844 toll free; outside Australia 61 2 9394 7600; fax: 61 2 9394 7601; email: memberservices@copyright.com.au

COPYING FOR OTHER PURPOSES

Except as permitted under the Act, for example a fair dealing for the purposes of study, research, criticism or review, no part of this book may be reproduced, stored in a retrieval system, or transmitted in any form or by any means without prior written permission. All enquiries should be made to the publisher at the address above.
Any performance or public reading of *That's One Damn Sexy Ape* is forbidden unless a licence has been received from the author or the author's agent. The purchase of this book in no way gives the purchaser the right to perform the play in public, whether by means of a staged production or a reading. All applications for public performance should be addressed to the author c/—Currency Press

Typeset by Brighton Gray for Currency Press.
Cover image by Ivan Jeldres.
Cover design Mathias Johansson.

Currency Press acknowledges the Traditional Owners of the Country on which we live and work. We pay our respects to all Aboriginal and Torres Strait Islander Elders, past and present.

A catalogue record for this book is available from the National Library of Australia

Contents

THAT'S ONE DAMN SEXY APE 1

Theatre Program at the end of the playtext

That's One Damn Sexy Ape was first produced by Gavin Roach Presents at La Mama Courthouse as part of the Melbourne International Comedy Festival, on the traditional Lands of the people of the Kulin Nation, Melbourne, on 16 April 2024, with the following cast and creatives:

ZOO ADMINISTRATOR	Perri Cummings
ZOO EMPLOYEE	Rupert Bevan
PR AGENT 1	Dax Carnay
PR AGENT 2	Asher Griffith-Jones
JOURNALISTS	Eleni Vettos and Jasper Jordan
BUBO THE GORILLA	Christopher Trimarchi

Director, Gavin Roach
Lighting Designer, Ashleigh Shearman
Set Designer, Fernando Ulloa
Sound Designer, Anthony Jacobsen
Stage Manager, Lowana van Dorssen

CHARACTERS

ZOO ADMINISTRATOR
ZOO EMPLOYEE
PR AGENT 1
PR AGENT 2
JOURNALIST
BUBO THE GORILLA

NOTES

Character names, race, pronouns and gender have been purposely left ambiguous to allow the creative team freedom to cast the play according to their artistic vision.

Bubo is to be played by an actor wearing tight, form-fitting blacks. He is on stage the entire time, in a small but detailed enclosure.

This play text went to press before the end of rehearsals and may differ from the play as performed.

SCENE 1: THE INTERVIEW

A harsh spotlight shines on the ZOO EMPLOYEE *centre stage, they look panicked and exhausted. After a moment of silence, the murmuring of a crowd can be heard as the* JOURNALIST *begins to ask their questions.*

JOURNALIST: Can you give us any indication as to how the child came to be in Bubo's enclosure?

ZOO EMPLOYEE: At this stage we are still looking into the exact way that the child was able to—

JOURNALIST: Is there any update on the child's condition?

ZOO EMPLOYEE: That is a question I'm not comfortable answering, out of respect to him and his parents—

JOURNALIST: But can you confirm that the child lost an arm? Some witness report that the gorilla dislodged and then ripped off the young boy's—

ZOO EMPLOYEE: Oh, come on, that is entirely not true. It didn't happen. The child did not lose his arm. His injuries were minor—

JOURNALIST: I would hardly call multiple fractures and a head wound 'minor'.

ZOO EMPLOYEE: What I mean is, given what could have happened—

JOURNALIST: Has Bubo ever displayed this level of aggression before?

ZOO EMPLOYEE: Bubo has never really had to deal with an unexpected individual in his surroundings before, so that is a bit of an unfair judgement—

JOURNALIST: So, this could have been avoided?

ZOO EMPLOYEE: Yes. With better supervision from his parents, that boy would never have—

JOURNALIST: So, you blame the parents then?

ZOO EMPLOYEE: Yes … wait, no. Look, I don't blame anyone—

JOURNALIST: But whose decision was it to use tranquillisers in such a high-risk situation?
ZOO EMPLOYEE: That was my call to make. It was a high-risk situation, for both the child and Bubo—
JOURNALIST: Can you elaborate on that?
ZOO EMPLOYEE: Given that Bubo had already lost interest and moved away from the boy, I was able to use a tranquilliser dart to knock Bubo out and then, we could get to the child.
JOURNALIST: But surely the child's safety was still at risk?
ZOO EMPLOYEE: We were lucky, with the child being unconscious he was less likely to startle Bubo and cause him any further distress—
JOURNALIST: Lucky?
ZOO EMPLOYEE: What I meant to say is—
JOURNALIST: Are you suggesting that you put the needs of a gorilla above the needs of a heavily wounded child?
ZOO EMPLOYEE: No that is not what I am saying at all—
JOURNALIST: One final question, what happens now?

> *The murmuring of the crowd grows and a few camera flashes go off.*

ZOO EMPLOYEE: I … I don't know …

> *Snap to black. Lights up on* BUBO THE GORILLA, *lounging in his enclosure. He is basking in the sunlight. His movements and gestures aren't overt but there is a subtle sexiness to him.*

SCENE 2: THE BOARDROOM

The ZOO ADMINISTRATOR, PR AGENT 1 *and* PR AGENT 2 *are sitting around the table, casually chatting.* ZOO EMPLOYEE *enters.*

ZOO EMPLOYEE: Sorry I'm late, I was—
PR AGENT 2: Doing your job.
PR AGENT 1: No need to apologise.
PR AGENT 2: Professionalism is rare these days.
PR AGENT 1: Almost unheard of.

    Silence.

Thirsty?
ZOO EMPLOYEE: Sorry?
PR AGENT 2: Water? Do you need water?
ZOO EMPLOYEE: No. Thank you.

    Silence.

I'm not being fired, am I?
PR AGENT 1: Being fired, ha, I like this one.

    Silence.

PR AGENT 2: Well, shall we—
ZOO ADMINISTRATOR: Right, of course, let's get down to business—
ZOO EMPLOYEE: Christ, I am being fired, aren't I?
PR AGENT 1: Babe, you have nothing to worry about—
ZOO EMPLOYEE: Please don't ever refer to me as 'babe' again.
PR AGENT 2: I couldn't be more sorry.
PR AGENT 1: It'll never happen again.
PR AGENT 2: Whacked it in the mental notebook.

    Silence.

PR AGENT 1: I think it's best if we get right to the point.
PR AGENT 2: Right, so … the incident …
ZOO EMPLOYEE: Shit.

Silence.

So—

ZOO ADMINISTRATOR: Keeping in mind the situation the zoo now finds itself in regarding what happens with—

PR AGENT 2: The gorilla—

PR AGENT 1: And, you—

ZOO ADMINISTRATOR: The board feels that we need to act quickly to—

PR AGENT 1: Soothe the masses—

ZOO ADMINISTRATOR: And take ownership of what happened, to—

PR AGENT 2: Shift focus—

PR AGENT 1: Re-invent—

PR AGENT 2: To make new—

PR AGENT 1: To move on from all this, unpleasantness—

PR AGENT 2: And rapidly.

ZOO ADMINISTRATOR: With the furore that has been whipped up by the press and with public opinion rather divided on how you … n how the zoo handled the situation, the board wants to ensure that, going forward, the zoo's most popular exhibit remains just as popular … after the dust settles—

PR AGENT 1: And that is where we come in.

PR AGENT 2: We specialise in situations, like this one—

PR AGENT 1: Sticky situations.

PR AGENT 2: Murky situations.

PR AGENT 2: Situations that are best brushed under the carpet—

PR AGENT 1: Just as quickly as they arise.

Silence.

ZOO EMPLOYEE: Okay—

PR AGENT 2: Okay.

Silence.

PR AGENT 1: Okay, I'm going to speed this up—

ZOO EMPLOYEE: I'm sorry?

PR AGENT 2: The gorilla—

ZOO EMPLOYEE: Which one?

PR AGENT 1: The big one—
PR AGENT 2: The male—
PR AGENT 1: The one who, did the … to the child—
ZOO EMPLOYEE: Bubo?
ZOO ADMINISTRATOR: Yes, Bubo.
ZOO EMPLOYEE: What about him?
PR AGENT 2: You mean, you haven't noticed?
PR AGENT 1: Not even in the hue of the setting sun?
ZOO EMPLOYEE: Noticed what?
PR AGENT 1: He's hot.
PR AGENT 2: Sexy.
PR AGENT 1: Primal.
ZOO ADMINISTRATOR: Masculine.
PR AGENT 1: Please don't box Bubo in with your heteronormative gender-biased language.
ZOO ADMINISTRATOR: I didn't realise that I was—
PR AGENT 1: Well, you are, you did, and it's offensive.
ZOO ADMINISTRATOR: I'm … sorry—
PR AGENT 1: Thank you.
ZOO EMPLOYEE: Can someone please tell me what the hell is happening?

> PR AGENT 1 *opens the laptop on the desk and starts typing.*

PR AGENT 1: Are you aware of the gorilla's unique celebrity status online?
ZOO EMPLOYEE: I kinda just assumed the internet would blow up over … what happened … so, I've been avoiding going online or reading any comments that—

> PR AGENT 1 *turns the laptop to face the* ZOO EMPLOYEE.

Is that … that's Bubo.
ZOO ADMINISTRATOR: A friend of mine sent me a link to that blog … well before what happened to that little boy, happened. I thought nothing of it, I thought it was a bit of a piss-take to be honest, but it turns out these people are serious. I looked into it a bit further and then I started looking at the sales figures and

how long this blog has been operating and it turns out, there is some pretty interesting data around Bubo's ... appeal.

PR AGENT 1: Which gives us an exciting opportunity—

PR AGENT 2: Like a new spring morning—

PR AGENT 1: Or a freshly birthed calf—

PR AGENT 2: Jesus, risen on the third day.

ZOO EMPLOYEE: So okay ... these women ...

PR AGENT 2: It's not just women—

ZOO ADMINISTRATOR: But they are actually fantasising over—

PR AGENT 2: Bubo—

PR AGENT 1: The gorilla.

PR AGENT 2: The sexy gorilla.

ZOO EMPLOYEE: Oh, come on, this can't be serious. He's an ape. An ape.

PR AGENT 1: Already in the past month alone, the number of contributors to the blog has doubled.

PR AGENT 2: And even with Bubo's more, aggressive tendencies—

ZOO ADMINISTRATOR: I wouldn't say aggressive—

PR AGENT 2: Our support for him has not wavered.

ZOO EMPLOYEE: Okay, but—

PR AGENT 1: What?

ZOO EMPLOYEE: He's an ape.

ZOO ADMINISTRATOR: Look, I agree, it's all a bit—

ZOO EMPLOYEE: Creepy.

PR AGENT 2: Creepy?

PR AGENT 1: Creepy is a little unfair. Is it creepy to be taken in by the mystique and exotic gaze of this majestic beast? Is it creepy to give yourself over to naive innocence? Is it creepy to indulge in a taboo fantasy? It is creepy to—

ZOO EMPLOYEE: Yes!

PR AGENT 2: Clearly you are crippled by a deep sense of shame—

ZOO EMPLOYEE: Look, it is one thing to be fascinated with Bubo as an animal but ... I mean ... read that one—

PR AGENT 1: Oooft, I'm going to need a drink after that.

ZOO EMPLOYEE: This is ridiculous!

ZOO ADMINISTRATOR: I know it's not exactly conventional, but this gives the zoo a unique opportunity, if—

PR AGENT 2: We strike now, while the iron's hot—

ZOO ADMINISTRATOR: And appropriately integrate Bubo's more positive qualities into the zoo's marketing strategies to potentially nullify his current negative image.

PR AGENT 1: And that's where you come in.

PR AGENT 2: We need you to make sure that Bubo maintains his, sexiness.

ZOO EMPLOYEE: His sexiness?

PR AGENT 1: For this strategy to work, Bubo has to stay, alluring.

PR AGENT 2: He already has a brooding mystic about him, but we need you to train him to—

ZOO EMPLOYEE: Okay no, I'm not his trainer and Bubo is not some circus monkey. Our relationship is strictly arm's length and will remain so. What happened was tragic, yes and should have been avoidable but this; making him out to be some kind of sex symbol ... no I don't want any part in ... whatever this is.

Silence.

ZOO ADMINISTRATOR: There have been a few people ... not many ... just a few ... and certainly not me ... who are questioning your continued employment with the zoo—

ZOO EMPLOYEE: I see.

Silence.

PR AGENT 1: Think it over.

ZOO EMPLOYEE: I don't need to.

PR AGENT 2: You don't need to answer right away.

ZOO EMPLOYEE: I think I just did.

PR AGENT 1: I would have thought you would be more willing to help, after all it was you who pulled the trigger, wasn't it?

PR AGENT 2: And you weren't exactly, pleasant, in front of the cameras—

ZOO EMPLOYEE: I was ambushed. I hadn't been briefed on what I could and couldn't say. I was tired and ... and I'd just pulled a child out from ... and ... I made a call and I stand by it. How much longer am I going to be punished for doing my job—?

Silence.

I need get back to work.

PR AGENT 2: We'll be in touch.

PR AGENT 1: Oh, and one more thing.

ZOO EMPLOYEE: What?!

PR AGENT 1: Circus ape.

ZOO EMPLOYEE: Excuse me—

PR AGENT 1: I'm sure you meant to say that Bubo isn't a circus ape, rather than a circus monkey. There is a difference.

ZOO EMPLOYEE *exits.*

I think that went well.

PR AGENT 2: Utterly splendid.

Snap to black.

SCENE 3: BUBO'S ENCLOSURE

BUBO *is lazing in the hot sun. His movements and gestures have a subtle sexiness to them.* ZOO EMPLOYEE *enters with a broom, dustpan and a bucket of frozen watermelon. They begin to sweep the stage until* BUBO *catches their eye.*

ZOO EMPLOYEE: You know you could help me rather than just sitting there.

> ZOO EMPLOYEE *continues to sweep as* BUBO *approaches the barrier.*

Oh, you want to know what's in the bucket, hey?

> ZOO EMPLOYEE *playfully teases* BUBO *with the bucket.*

What could it be?

> BUBO *begins to play along.*

Maybe apples? Or a banana? Rockmelon?

> PR AGENT 1 *enters unnoticed.*

One last guess?

> ZOO EMPLOYEE *removes pieces of watermelon from the bucket and throws them over to* BUBO.

Go on … go get it.

> ZOO EMPLOYEE *throws more as* BUBO *races around the enclosure gathering up the pieces of watermelon.*

Who's a sexy ape? Who's a sexy, sexy ape?
PR AGENT 1: Does he ever answer back?

> ZOO EMPLOYEE *screams, startled.*

Sorry—
ZOO EMPLOYEE: Don't sneak up on me like that.
PR AGENT 1: Sorry, I would have said something sooner but you have a real connection with him—

ZOO EMPLOYEE: It's the watermelon. It's his favourite.
PR AGENT 1: I see.

Silence.

I wanted to apologise, for the other day.
ZOO EMPLOYEE: Okay.
PR AGENT 1: We came on a little heavy-handed.
ZOO EMPLOYEE: Look, it's—
PR AGENT 1: But that's our job. I'm just trying to do my job.
ZOO EMPLOYEE: I get it.

Silence.

PR AGENT 1: Okay … let's start again … how long have you been with the zoo?
ZOO EMPLOYEE: Around fifteen years. Seven as a keeper though. I spent my first few years volunteering and then, when I was studying at university, I worked in the café, and then the gift shop, and then, anywhere they'd let me. I was happy to just be here.
PR AGENT 1: And are you still just as happy?
ZOO EMPLOYEE: Um, well, recent events aside, yeah … yeah, I am. I mean the admin side of things is a bit shit and some days you have to deal with—
PR AGENT 1: Brash public-relations freelancers?
ZOO EMPLOYEE: Exactly, but then I get to come and throw frozen watermelon at a gorilla. Not many people can say that that is in their job description.
PR AGENT 1: And did you always want to work with Bubo?
ZOO EMPLOYEE: Oh no, I when I started here, I wanted to work with the pachyderms. The elephants.
PR AGENT 1: But then how did you end up—
ZOO EMPLOYEE: Management. The primate team was down a keeper so I was shifted over.
PR AGENT 1: Right.
ZOO EMPLOYEE: But once I've paid my dues … and the elephants aren't going anywhere … those things live forever.

PR AGENT 1: But surely, you'd miss him. I mean, look at that face.
ZOO EMPLOYEE: Yeah, I'd miss him. My big idiot. I'd miss them all. You get attached. You can't help it. You try to stay objective and maintain an 'it's just a job' mentality but then you start to picking up on all their little mannerisms. Their little quirks and soon, you get sucked in. When you watch them, actually it's when you're not watching them, when something catches your eye, just in the corner, like you see the young ones playing or a mother cradling her newborn or even just Bubo watching his herd, you know that there is something going on, something more you will never understand. Something you're not ever meant to understand.

    ZOO EMPLOYEE *notices* PR AGENT 1 *making notes and stops.*

PR AGENT 1: No, no, that was good, very good … I can use that.
ZOO EMPLOYEE: I have to get back to—

    ZOO EMPLOYEE *begins to exit.*

They aren't pets, you know. They aren't your family … they aren't your friends. It's best you remember that. The greatest act of respect we ever granted them was to build that barrier.
PR AGENT 1: To keep them in—
ZOO EMPLOYEE: It keeps us out.

    ZOO EMPLOYEE *exits.* PR AGENT 1 *turns and stares at* BUBO.

SCENE 4: ADVERTISEMENT

Spotlight on BUBO, *music begins to swell: Billie Eilish's 'Bad Guy' plays as* BUBO *poses and twerks. A sultry voiceover begins to speak.*

VOICEOVER: Strong.
    Virile.
    Tough.
    Musky.
    He's a bad boy.
    The weather isn't the only thing that's heating up.
    There's never been a better time to feast your eyes on one of nature's finest specimens.
    So, what are you waiting for?
    Zoos aren't just for kids anymore.

    BUBO *continues to pose as the music throbs and lights fade.*

SCENE 5: BUBO'S ENCLOSURE

BUBO *laying in his enclosure. He is visibly wounded and there is a vulnerability to his movements.*

PR AGENT 1: What's happened?

PR AGENT 2: Oh God, is he okay? Can someone tell me if he is okay—?

> PR AGENT 2 *sees the full extent of* BUBO*'s injuries as they collapse to the ground in horror.*

No!

PR AGENT 1: Christ, pop a Valium—

> ZOO ADMINISTRATOR *enters.*

What the hell is this?

ZOO ADMINISTRATOR: I've been told it's not as bad as it looks.

PR AGENT 1: Not as bad … not as bad …

> PR AGENT 1 *takes out a cigarette packet.*

ZOO ADMINISTRATOR: You can't smoke here—

PR AGENT 1: Okay—

> PR AGENT 1 *tries to light the cigarette.*

ZOO ADMINISTRATOR: No really, this is a non-smoking—

PR AGENT 1: Got it.

> PR AGENT 1 *lights the cigarette.*

ZOO ADMINISTRATOR: So, put it out—

PR AGENT 1: I'm going to need you to back up out of my personal space, okay? I am stressed and rapidly approaching breaking point and you do not want to be around when I crack.

PR AGENT 2: You really don't—

> ZOO EMPLOYEE *enters.*

ZOO EMPLOYEE: Okay, so I've been informed that, um, you can't smoke here—

PR AGENT 1 *glares at* ZOO EMPLOYEE, *takes a long slow drag on their cigarette, blows out the smoke and then puts it out.*

PR AGENT 2: What … happened?

ZOO EMPLOYEE: There was a fight—

PR AGENT 2: Oh God.

ZOO EMPLOYEE: Bubo took a pretty bad beating. Judging from what the keepers saw, his son Chimly challenged him for the alpha of the herd and they fought—

PR AGENT 2: Judas.

PR AGENT 1: And?

ZOO EMPLOYEE: And in the wild they'd be able to maintain some distance but with such a confined environment, Bubo had nowhere to go, so the fight lasted longer than usual and—

PR AGENT 1: And what? What does any of this mean?

ZOO EMPLOYEE: It means that Bubo is no longer the alpha. It happens, he's old and weakening, so—

PR AGENT 2: How dare you—

ZOO EMPLOYEE: This is very common, the young challenge the old and eventually the old either die in the fight or move on, and then die, on their own.

PR AGENT 1: But he lived, Bubo lived, so he can challenge him again. He can fight back. Reclaim what is his—

ZOO EMPLOYEE: No, it doesn't work like that. When this happens in captivity the losing alpha has to be moved—

PR AGENT 1: Moved? You would move Bubo?

ZOO EMPLOYEE: Yes, once we find him a new home—

PR AGENT 2: This is his home.

ZOO EMPLOYEE: Not any more—

PR AGENT 1: This is a disaster.

ZOO ADMINISTRATOR: Look it's not great timing, I know and we are all clearly upset by the situation, but—

PR AGENT 1: The situation? The situation? Let me tell you what the situation here is. The situation here is that our star attraction, our major selling point, has just been beaten within an inch of

his life. Just look at him. No sexy gorilla means no hype, and no hype means no customers, and no customers means … is any of this making sense to you yet?
PR AGENT 2: We can fix this. We can spin it. Um, strong proud gorilla gets challenged—
PR AGENT 1: Ambushed—
PR AGENT 2: Usurped—
PR AGENT 1: By his own son—
PR AGENT 2: *Hamlet*. Tragedy. It's very Shakespearian—
PR AGENT 1: Lesser male exerts his dominance in a cruel grasp for power—
ZOO EMPLOYEE: Um, technically Bubo is now the lesser.
PR AGENT 1: I'm going to pretend I didn't hear that—
PR AGENT 2: He's wounded in battle—
PR AGENT 1: Like a proud solider returning from war—
PR AGENT 2: Racked with the scars of combat—
PR AGENT 1: Scars are sexy—
PR AGENT 2: Women love a man with scars—
ZOO EMPLOYEE: He's not a man … he's a primate—
PR AGENT 1: Still can't hear you—
PR AGENT 2: We can track his recovery—
PR AGENT 1: Hashtag: Pray for Bubo—
PR AGENT 2: Yes!
PR AGENT 1: Okay … okay. It is going to be okay.
ZOO ADMINISTRATOR: Maybe we should put the brakes on the campaign, just until we know more.
ZOO EMPLOYEE: And now there's Chimly. I mean, if you need a primate to focus on, why not focus on him? He is the new alpha after all.
PR AGENT 1: Listening again.
ZOO EMPLOYEE: And he is Bubo's son—
PR AGENT 2: Fresh new blood—
PR AGENT 1: A younger man—
PR AGENT 2: Virile. Athletic—
PR AGENT 1: Strong—

PR AGENT 2: Sweaty—
ZOO EMPLOYEE: Sweaty?
PR AGENT 1: Which one is this … Chimly?
ZOO EMPLOYEE: He's that one, over there, up on the rock. We call it Pride Rock because it looks like—

    PR AGENT 1 *and* PR AGENT 2 *stare into the enclosure.*

PR AGENT 1: What the hell is that?
PR AGENT 2: Oh God … evil has a face!
PR AGENT 1: I think I'm going to be sick.
ZOO ADMINISTRATOR: I think maybe we all need to calm down—
PR AGENT 1: Calm down? Calm down? That … thing … is hideous.
ZOO EMPLOYEE: Hey!
PR AGENT 2: I can't even—
PR AGENT 1: That thing is the new—
ZOO EMPLOYEE: Alpha? Yes.
PR AGENT 1: And the, herd or whatever, is okay with that?
ZOO EMPLOYEE: He proved himself to be stronger than Bubo, so—
PR AGENT 2: Nope … not buying it.
PR AGENT 1: Send him away. That one. That thing. Look at it. Evil. Pure, cold, unadulterated savagery.
PR AGENT 2: Can you make it look away? I can't deal with it staring at me, with its cold dead eyes—
ZOO EMPLOYEE: Okay, well, I think there's nothing more to discuss—
PR AGENT 1: Oh, we aren't finished—
ZOO EMPLOYEE: No, I am. Look it's been fun … not really but … it was … yeah—

    ZOO EMPLOYEE *exits.*

PR AGENT 1: I don't know what you need to do to fix this situation, but fix it.
PR AGENT 2: Got that? Fix this.

    PR AGENT 1 *and* PR AGENT 2 *exit.*

SCENE 6: THE STATEMENT

A harsh spotlight shines on the ZOO ADMINISTRATOR *centre stage. They look panicked and exhausted. The murmuring of a crowd can be heard.*

ZOO ADMINISTRATOR: All right, thank you all for coming out today, I won't keep you long. I'll be making a brief statement and then I will have time for a few questions, and a few questions only.

On the twelfth of this month the zoo's large silverback gorilla, Bubo, was involved in an incident with his son, Chimly, this resulted in Bubo sustaining a number of serious but not life-threating injuries. Chimly was isolated from the herd while Bubo recovered and thankfully Bubo made a swift and full recovery.

Unfortunately, this was not, as we feared, an isolated incident. Upon returning to the herd, Chimly again challenged Bubo for dominance and this second attack left Bubo with not only scratches and deep bite marks, but also a broken right arm and fractured jaw. Bubo has been attended to and will be kept away from the herd until he has stabilised.

What this means moving forward, however, is that, for the good of the herd and the health of the two males involved, we will be sending Bubo to our sister zoo in Tokyo, where he will live out the remainder of his, no doubt long life, in a specially built facility that caters for older gorillas that need some extra care in their later years.

This was not an easy decision to make. Bubo has been part of the zoo family since his birth and we have all grown to love and care for him, just as many of our visitors have. The decision to relocate Bubo and not Chimly was based purely in keeping with the zoo's best-practice measures. To put it simply, Chimly challenged Bubo for dominance of the herd and won, making him the new alpha. This appears to be accepted by the rest of the herd and so, if we were to interfere and upset this new hierarchy structure, for the sake of favouring our old friend, then we would be doing more harm than good.

Rest assured Bubo will still be around for a little while longer. As you can imagine, the logistics of a cross-continent relocation will take a lot of planning and we are determined to get it right. In the meantime, we urge our visitors to come down, say their final goodbye to Bubo, and take in all that the zoo has on offer.

The ZOO ADMINISTRATOR *folds away the statement as the swell of the crowd increase.*

JOURNALIST: Does this relocation have anything to do with the incident that occurred with the small boy, especially considering his parents filed a class-action lawsuit against the zoo only this morning?

ZOO ADMINISTRATOR: The timing of Bubo's relocation has nothing to do with the unfortunate events involving the young boy and his family. The zoo is assisting investigators with their inquires and we are confident that this matter will be settled in due course.

JOURNALIST: Is there any truth to the allegations that this arrangement is a stunt to distract from the recent disastrous social media campaign that saw the zoo facing widespread backlash?

ZOO ADMINISTRATOR: I am not sure where these accusations have come from but I can assure you that there is absolutely no truth to that statement whatsoever.

JOURNALIST: But you do acknowledge that in hyper-sexualising Bubo, the zoo made a mistake?

ZOO ADMINISTRATOR: Although the zoo acknowledges that its social media presence is constantly changing and evolving in line with innovative marketing practices and trends, we were, this time, naively led astray, and placed far too much trust in individuals who did not deliver on expectation. We are sorry for any offence caused and we look forward to returning to what we do best, welcoming our visitors and educating them on the many, many species we have here at the zoo. I think it's best that we leave the social media arena to those who know what they are doing.

Laughter.

JOURNALIST: Just one more question—

ZOO ADMINISTRATOR: I think that about wraps things up for today—

JOURNALIST: But what about the employee who shot Bubo?

ZOO ADMINISTRATOR: Excuse me?

JOURNALIST: Well, they are still here, working; I saw them on the grounds when I arrived this morning.

ZOO ADMINISTRATOR: I'm not sure I'm following.

JOURNALIST: I just question why an employee, who quite literally shot one of the zoo's main attractions and is now embroiled in a rather high-profile lawsuit, why have they been allowed to not only keep their job, but from what I saw, they still have access to a number of authorized only areas ... specifically where the firearms are kept. It's almost as if, they got away with it.

The crowd begins to rumble and cameras flash as the lights fade down.

SCENE 7: BUBO'S ENCLOSURE

BUBO *lazing in the sun, he is content and sexy. The* ZOO EMPLOYEE *is mopping the area in front of the enclosure. Slowly* PR AGENT 1 *enters.*

PR AGENT 1: I thought I'd find you here.
ZOO EMPLOYEE: Christ! Don't sneak up on someone like that.
PR AGENT 1: Sorry.
ZOO EMPLOYEE: God, my heart is racing. Seriously, do you make a sound at all when you walk?
PR AGENT 1: What can I say, it's a gift.
ZOO EMPLOYEE: Well, try to be a little more heavy-footed around me thanks.
PR AGENT 1: Noted.

Silence.

I wanted to come and say goodbye.
ZOO EMPLOYEE: Right. Okay.
PR AGENT 1: I know we kind of got off on the wrong foot, but I really enjoyed—
ZOO EMPLOYEE: I didn't exactly make things easy for you. You were just doing your job and I—
PR AGENT 1: Well, we barrelled in and caught you off guard and—

Silence.

ZOO EMPLOYEE: So, you got fired hey?
PR AGENT 1: Yup.
ZOO EMPLOYEE: For what it's worth, it was a pretty good campaign.
PR AGENT 1: Really?
ZOO EMPLOYEE: Oh, the ideas were terrible. Truly … awful, but the production values were really impressive.
PR AGENT 1: Well, that's something, I guess.

Silence.

So, what's next for you? Back to looking after the herd and … Chimly? Shame you can't go with this big guy to Tokyo.

ZOO EMPLOYEE: This is actually my last week with the primates. I start with the reptiles on Monday.

PR AGENT 1: Promotion?

ZOO EMPLOYEE: Punishment. It's darker and there's less chance of me being seen … or shooting anything.

PR AGENT 1: Oh …

ZOO EMPLOYEE: And I really fucking hate reptiles too. Slimy, scaly, evil-looking things. I swear they are just waiting to attack, watching you with their beady little eyes.

PR AGENT 1: So, they really choose the right person for the job then—

ZOO EMPLOYEE: Hey, you can talk.

PR AGENT 1: Ouch!

ZOO EMPLOYEE: What will you do now?

PR AGENT 1: On to the next job, I don't mourn my failures.

ZOO EMPLOYEE: I wouldn't call it a failure.

PR AGENT 1: I would.

ZOO EMPLOYEE: Okay. Well … it was good to meet you.

> ZOO EMPLOYEE *puts out their hand to shake.* PR AGENT 1 *hesitates a moment and then shakes their hand.*

PR AGENT 1: Good to meet you too.

ZOO EMPLOYEE: I grabbed the wrong gun.

PR AGENT 1: Sorry?

ZOO EMPLOYEE: When I shot Bubo, I grabbed the wrong gun.

PR AGENT 1: I don't understand.

ZOO EMPLOYEE: I have to tell someone and well …you're going … and for some reason I trust you …and it's been just …when it happened, when the boy fell in, I honestly froze. All my training went out the window and I just stood there, staring at this kid laying in the enclosure. Nothing seemed to move me, not the screams or even the people rushing past me to help. When I finally did, when I finally snapped out of it and moved, it was like I was trying to catch up with what was happening, get back some semblance of control.

I wasn't thinking clearly and I when I got to the guns cage, I just grabbed one, I don't even think that I paid too much attention to what I was actually grabbing, I just knew that I needed to get a gun.

And we've all been lying, the zoo, the administrators, me, all of us. We were way behind on routine checks and the cage wasn't even locked and the gun I picked up wasn't in the right spot and worse …it was loaded—

PR AGENT 1: But you used a trank gun, you tranquillised Bubo.

ZOO EMPLOYEE: See, I thought I had grabbed a rifle … all my training told me to grab a rifle … and I just assumed it was loaded … I hoped it was loaded … I was running on pure adrenaline by then.

And when I finally got through the crowd … when I found a clear shot … I … I aimed the gun at the kid.

My first thought … my only thought was … well … the kid should die. Here's this kid, this kid who's wandered off from his parents or just been blatantly ignored and has ended up in the one place that he really shouldn't be and … and all my training tells me to shoot the animal, to shoot Bubo, who's done nothing wrong, mind you, who has just been going about his day, doing his own thing in this tiny world we have locked him in, and now this kid, this kid invades his nothing of an existence and he is the one who has to die?

I wanted so much to pull the trigger, to just say that the gun pulled to the left and take the shot. The kid would be dead, sure, but Bubo would be alive.

I could feel the pressure build in my fingertip and then … I swung the gun to the right, aimed at Bubo, breathed out and fired, fully thinking that this would be the bullet that kills an endangered silverback gorilla. It was only when I saw the flash of red sticking out of his neck that I realised I had grabbed the wrong gun.

The rest … what happened next … was just … luck. Bubo moved away from the kid, the dart was a strong tranquilliser and no-one had to die. I'd done my job.

But while everyone was celebrating getting the boy out

safely ... I just stood there, staring at Bubo, thinking ... 'Wow, I almost shot a kid today'—

> PR AGENT 2 *is suddenly seen inside the enclosure with* BUBO. *They are in their underwear and very slowly approaching* BUBO *with open arms.*

PR AGENT 1: Oh Jesus Christ!

ZOO EMPLOYEE: I've made peace it ... what I did ... what I could have done—

PR AGENT 1: What the fuck are you doing?

ZOO EMPLOYEE: Um ... I'm trying to open up to you—

PR AGENT 1: No! Turn the fuck around.

ZOO EMPLOYEE: Shit! What the hell are you doing? Get out of there!

PR AGENT 2: I can't do that, not until I know.

PR AGENT 1: Are you insane? Get the hell out of there!

PR AGENT 2: It's okay; he's not going to hurt me.

ZOO EMPLOYEE: Just back away really slowly ... really slowly ... don't turn your back ... okay ... just one foot behind the next ... really slow.

PR AGENT 1: Shoot it! Shoot the goddamn thing.

ZOO EMPLOYEE: Keep your voice down! If Bubo gets agitated this is not going to end well.

> PR AGENT 2 *moves closer to* BUBO, *who has started to pace in their corner.*

Stay here ... get them to back up ... don't make any sudden movements.

PR AGENT 1: Just move!

> ZOO EMPLOYEE *exits.*

What the fuck are you playing at?!

PR AGENT 2: I love him. From the first moment I saw him I fell under his spell. I tried to fight it but why deny myself a chance at happiness? A chance at love?

PR AGENT 1: It's a fucking monkey!

PR AGENT 2: Ape, he's an ape; and you know that. I don't expect you to understand, but I can feel it, a connection, between him and I. It's stronger than just physical, it's deeper, it's … it's like the whole world has washed away and it's just him and I left. Oh god, you should smell his musk.

PR AGENT 1: This is crazy.

PR AGENT 2: I can't let him leave, not without knowing that I love him.

PR AGENT 1: Just listen to yourself! You don't love him; you're just having an acute psychological episode and it's causing you to project your feelings onto this monk … ape … onto Bubo. You don't love him … you're just, not well …

PR AGENT 2: Tell that to Sigourney Weaver!

PR AGENT 1: What?!

PR AGENT 2: Sigourney Weaver. Dian Fossey … *Gorillas in the* fucking *Mist*! How she didn't win every award for her performance in that movie, I will never know!

> PR AGENT 1 *stares in shock and confusion.*

People thought Dian Fossey was crazy … living out there … in the jungle … alone … with only the gorillas, but she wasn't crazy … and neither am I.

PR AGENT 1: Okay … okay … you can live out whatever fantasy this is but I need you to back up … just give Bubo some space, okay … Let him come to you.

PR AGENT 2: He won't hurt me, I'm not afraid.

PR AGENT 1: Just stand still … right there … don't move any closer …

> *Suddenly* BUBO *becomes more agitated, snorting and moving aggressively. Without warning* BUBO *rushes towards* PR AGENT 2.

Take it! Take the shot!

> *Blackout. A gunshot.* PR AGENT 1 *screams.*

THE END

That's One Damn Sexy Ape

written by **Gavin Roach**

April 16 - April 21, 2024 at La Mama Courthouse as part of the Melbourne International Comedy Festival

Zoo Administrator: Perri Cummings
Zoe Employee: Rupert Bevan
PR Agent 1: Dax Carnay
PR Agent 2: Asher Griffith-Jones
Journalists: Eleni Vettos and Jasper Jordan
Bubo the Gorilla: Christopher Trimarchi

Director, Gavin Roach
Lighting Designer, Ashleigh Shearman
Set Design, Fernando Ulloa
Sound Design, Anthony Jacobsen
Stage Manager, Lowana van Dorssen

LA MAMA THEATRE: FACILITATING FEARLESSLY INDEPENDENT THEATRE-MAKING.

Founded in 1967, La Mama is Australia's most vital, responsive, inclusive and diverse home of independent theatre-making. We believe in the power and possibilities of theatre and art for all people.

La Mama engages audiences as a community and offers affordable and hospitable cultural experiences that appeal to a broad range of people.

Each year at La Mama, two thousand artists develop their practice, are given their first opportunity and have their finest performance moment. Hundreds of new Australian works have been generated over the decades.

Annually we present 40+ Australian premieres, participate in festivals (Midsumma, Comedy, Fringe, Yirramboi) and present our own festivals & programs: First Nations, Festival of Mother Tongue (LOTE), Puppet Festival, quarterly children and multi-arts (poetry, cabaret, music, scratch), Explorations (works in development), Emerge (Youth), Online and Pathways.

We exist to nurture and amplify all Australian voices.

Photograhs by Glenn Hester Photography

GAVIN ROACH
PLAYWRIGHT / DIRECTOR

Gavin Roach has a Bachelor of Arts (Acting for the Screen and Stage), Bachelor of Arts (Acting for the Screen and Stage, Honours) CSU, Masters in Arts Management UTS and Masters in Writing for Performance VCA.

Gavin is the writer, performer and producer of *Confessions of a Grindr Addict* (Sydney, Melbourne, Newcastle, Edinburgh, Perth Adelaide, Launceston, Hobart and New Zealand), *Any Womb Will Do* (Sydney, Melbourne and New Zealand), *I Can't Say The F Word* (Melbourne, Perth and New Zealand), *The Measure of a Man* (Melbourne, Sydney, Perth, Hobart, Brisbane and Prague), *All The Songs I Can't Sing* (Melbourne) and *Your Silence Will Not Protect You* (Melbourne, Sydney, Perth and Adelaide).

Gavin adapted and produced *Beyond Priscilla: The Play*, and was the co-devisor and co-creative developer of *We Were There*, showcasing the stories of women during the HIV/AIDS crisis in Australia.

Gavin's producing credits include *Manwatching*, *All I See Is You*, *The Loneliness Project*, *Adam*, *The Campaign*, *Sink*, *Transgression*, *Meet Me at Dawn*, *Pops*, *If We Got Some More Cocaine I Could Show You How I Love You*, *CULT*, *A Southern Fairytale*, *STUCK* and *Sauna Boy*. Gavin's producing and directing credits include *Lake Disappointment*, *Awkward Conversations With Animals I've Fucked*, *The Shy Manifesto*, *Run*, *Bottom*, *A Hundred Words For Snow*, *Heather*, *Disco Pigs*, *Outlier Peter Fechter: 59 Minutes*, *This Is Living*, *Bacon*, *One of Them Ones* and *Vespertilio*.

DAX CARNAY
PR AGENT 1

Dax has a rich heritage in the arts, rooted in their academic journey at the University of the Philippines. Since 2003, they have been an active member of the University of the Philippines Repertory Company, making significant strides as a cultural worker and activist within the theatre scene. Dax's contributions have spanned various roles, including actor, director, marketing consultant and producer, collaborating with esteemed organisations such as the Metro Manila Pride Organisation, Repertory Philippines, Philippine Educational Theater Association, Manila Fringe, Nineworks Theatrical, ABS-CBN, GMA, Dulaang UP, The Virgin Labfest, Cinemalaya, Cinefilipino, Cinemaone Originals, Tanghalang Pilipino, Cultural Center of the Philippines, and the International Theater Institute.

In 2020, Dax embarked on a new chapter in Melbourne, drawn by the city's vibrant cultural diversity and the opportunity to inspire others through their story. They immersed themselves in furthering their craft with dedication, undergoing training in the Meisner technique at Meisner Studio Manila, Screen Acting at the National Institute of Dramatic Art, and the National Actors Intensive at The Australian Film and Television Academy. Dax's commitment to excellence led them to be selected for the prestigious Malthouse Emerging Writers Program in 2023, an opportunity that allowed them to further hone their craft in writing for the stage.

In Melbourne, Dax continued to forge meaningful collaborations with groups, artists, and festivals, including the Melbourne International Comedy Festival, SBS, 24 Carrot

Productions, Eagle's Nest Theatre, Zanny Begg, La Mama Theatre, Western Edge, and Antipodes Theatre. This vibrant engagement with the local arts scene culminated in Dax being honoured as BroadwayWorld's Best Performer in a Play for Melbourne in 2023, a significant accolade that underscores their exceptional talent and the profound impact of their contributions to the theatre community in Melbourne.

ASHER GRIFFITH-JONES
PR AGENT 2

An Anglo-Indian Australian, Asher Griffith-Jones is a proud alumni of 16th Street Actors Studio. His recent work includes the 2023 productions of *If We Got Some More Cocaine I Could Show You How I Love You* directed by Christian Cavallo, the National Tour of *Mr Stink* directed by Jonathan Biggins, *One Of Them Ones* directed by Gavin Roach and just recently closed Melbourne Shakespeare Company's *Much Ado About Nothing* directed by Emma Austin. Asher is also a massive fan of cows. So, if you don't like the show, please 'moo' not 'boo'.

ELENI VETTOS
JOURNALIST

Eleni is thrilled to performing her first voiceover role in *That's One Damn Sexy Ape!* Originally from rural Victoria, Eleni is a graduate actor from Federation University Arts Academy (2014). Over the last five years, Eleni has been working in both the performing arts industry and education, across Victoria and the Northern Territory. Her most recent theatre credits include playing Portia in *The Merchant of Venice*, (Melbourne Shakespeare Company), and Chancellor / Magic Mirror in the musical/ comedy, *A Brutally Honest Fairy Tale* at the 2023 Melbourne Fringe Festival. Eleni also recently toured a production of *Love's Labour's Lost* with the Australian Shakespeare Company to the Stratford Shakespeare Festival and Prague Fringe Festival. Eleni is proudly represented by Ian Nisbet Talent Management and would like to thank Ian, Jess and her family and friends for the continuing support they've shown her through each of her theatrical pursuits.

JASPER JORDAN
JOURNALIST

Jasper is thrilled to be voicing a journalist in this production as he makes his debut at La Mama Theatre. He plays the supporting role of Spike in *Single Out* (season 2 onwards) and is part of the Early Career Artists Program running at Theatre Works in their August production of *The Volition Project*. He recently played Boyet in Australian Shakespeare Company's *Love's Labour's Lost* (2023) and has acted in upcoming feature films such as *Better Man*, *Freelance* and *CCTV Nasty*. He is currently studying for a Bachelor of Arts at the University of Melbourne and has previously completed the actor's studio at the National Institute of Dramatic Art (2022) and a Diploma of Theatre Arts at Melbourne Polytechnic (2021).

RUPERT BEVAN
ZOO EMPLOYEE

Since graduating from the VCA (BFA Acting), Rupert has continued to hone his craft in theatre, most recently in the acclaimed sold-out Australian premiere of *The Inheritance* at fortyfivedownstairs. Other highlights include *Away* at Theatre Works and *A Midsummer Night's Dream* for Sport For Jove in Sydney and the Blue Mountains. His one-man show, *DARLING BOY* (dir. Lucy Rossen), which he also wrote and produced, has enjoyed sold-out seasons in Melbourne, Sydney, and in 2023 it made its UK premiere to great acclaim at the Edinburgh Fringe Festival. *DARLING BOY* has been invited to perform in Dublin this year and Rupert will undertake training at Arthaus Berlin, as the recipient of the Keith and Elisabeth Murdoch Travelling Fellowship (Theatre) and assistance from the Ian Potter Cultural Trust. Rupert will next be seen on TV screens in *The Narrow Road to the Deep North* (Curio Pictures / Sony Pictures Television) on Amazon Prime, directed by Justin Kurzel (*Nitram*, *Snowtown*).

PERRI CUMMINGS
ZOO ADMINISTRATOR

Actor and writer Perri Cummings was a founding member of Tropic Line Theatre in Queensland, working and training with Jean Pierre Voos for seven years. In Melbourne, she has worked regularly in independent theatre and performed for two outdoor Shakespeare companies. Her recent theatre work includes *Then The Snow Fell On Egypt* by Gavin Roach and directed by Sarah Vickery, *The Association for Girls Act Good* (an immersive theatre piece she also wrote), *The Girlie Show*, directed and written by Wayne Tunks and *Coming Out*, written and directed by Scott Taylor. Her recent TV work includes *The Doctor Blake Mysteries*, *The Bazura Project*, *Conspiracy 360*, *Laid*, and played Jill Ramsay in *Neighbours*, where she has also worked as a Storyliner and Scriptwriter. She has also had major roles in two independent feature films, *Trench* and *Apparitions*, which she co-wrote, produced and directed as one half of the independent film company Cinema Viscera.

CHRISTOPHER TRIMARCHI
BUBO THE GORILLA

Chris is beyond excited to be playing Bubo the Gorilla in *That's One Damn Sexy Ape!*
With a Diploma in performing arts from 2005, Chris worked as a dancer for ten years with work spanning from TV appearances (AFL Footy Show Players review) and commercials (Goulburn Valley Gould), Video Clips (Ricki Lee—*Hell No*), Bollywood movies (*Salaam Namaste*), to stage (*Hollywood HonkyTonk* choreographed by Michael Ralph) and others including the AFL grand final half time show

behind *Kath and Kim*.

Working in between on board Princess Cruises, Chris then spent five years as resident rehearsal choreographer with Grayboy Entertainment for PnO Cruises Australia setting up the shows on board.

Chris now teaches Reformer Pilates at IR, leaving the dancing world behind, but is looking forward to settling into his enclosure at La Mama to premiere *That's One Damn Sexy Ape* bringing Bubo to life.

LOWANA VAN DORSSEN
STAGE MANAGER

Lowana is a graduate of the Victorian College of the Arts. During their final year of studies, she had the pleasure of interning with MTC (*Storm Boy* directed by Sam Strong), and Chunky Move (Token Armies, choreographed by Antony Hamilton). Post studies, Lowana has worked with Red Stitch (*Single Ladies*, dir. Bagryana Popov; *Prayer Machine*, dir. Krystalla Pierce; *The Amateurs*, dir. Susie Dee), Melbourne Opera (*Die Walküre*; *The Rise and Fall of the City of Mahagonny*; both dir. Suzanne Chaundy) and Three Fates Theatre (*Gundog*; dir. Alonso Pineda).

Most recently Lowana was the Deputy Stage Manager on the University of Melbournes production of Die Zauberflöte.

In her spare time Lowana enjoys film photography and typewriters.

Lowana is a proud member of the MEAA.

ANTHONY JACOBSEN
SOUND DESIGNER

Anthony is a versatile music producer, writer, and performer hailing from Brisbane, and boasts a rich background in the performing arts industry. His journey began as an independent music producer before composing for Channel 10's *Crocamole*, where he quickly garnered recognition.

Since then, Anthony has evolved into a prolific figure, contributing significantly to the realm of musical theatre through creating various productions including *Love After*, *Endings*, and his inaugural song cycle, *Struggling to Speak*. He also has credits as a theatrical sound designer, with his most recent credits including Taylor Made Productions' *Holding the Man* and *Torch Song*.

Academically, Anthony has acquired bachelor's degrees in Music from the Queensland University of Technology and Musical Theatre from the Fed Uni Arts Academy.

ASHLEIGH SHEARMAN
LIGHTING DESIGNER

Ashleigh Shearman is a trans theatre practitioner with over ten years experience in theatre as a performer, designer, and writer.

Originally from Gadigal Land, she has appeared in shows including *Dusty the Original Pop Diva* and *A Midsummer Night's Dream* both with St Vincent's Girls College, *HAIR* with Exclaim Theatre Company, *Witches of Eastwick* and *Urinetown* both with AIM, and *Little Shop of Horrors* with Rockdale Musical Society.

She has also provided lighting designs for *The Fantasticks* with Exclaim Theatre Company, the premiere of *Together Apart* by Nicholas Gentile, *Chicago* with AIM, *Dreamgirls* with Rockdale Musical Society, *The Gondoliers* with Rockdale Opera Company, *Cloud Nine* and *Baccarat* with VCA, and countless recitals, short form performances, and live events at AIM, with Birdie Productions, and as a freelance designer.

FERNANDO ULLOA
SET DESIGNER

Fernando Ulloa is an upcoming building designer who believes in the connection between spaces and emotions. He has been surrounded by the arts, and the world of theatre for the past 3 years, inspiring him more and more to be part of the magical creative process of it.

In 2023 Fernando was the Set Designer on *Peter Fetcher: 59 Minutes* (director Gavin Roach) during the Midsumma Festival.

www.currency.com.au

Visit Currency Press' website now to:
- Buy your books online
- Browse through our full list of titles, from plays to screenplays, books on theatre, film and music, and more
- Choose a play for your school or amateur performance group by cast size and gender
- Obtain information about performance rights
- Find out about theatre productions and other performing arts news across Australia
- For students, read our study guides
- For teachers, access syllabus and other relevant information
- Sign up for our email newsletter

The performing arts publisher

www.ingramcontent.com/pod-product-compliance
Lightning Source LLC
Chambersburg PA
CBHW050028090426
42734CB00021B/3472